IN THE NAME OF THE FATHER, THE SON, AND THE GRANDSON

By

Arthur Whittle
Ron Whittle
Jake Hansen

FORWARD

The title of the book came about as a culmination of the work of three family members who directly or indirectly wrote on their own. Arthur was my father and passed away a number of years ago. Everyone loved his sense of humor. Dad wrote the nursery rhymes for my sister's three daughters to keep them entertained when they were at his house.

I started writing when I was a senior for the high school newspaper. I enjoyed it a lot but I never really knew how to use my talents until I was on my way to Vietnam. I was in full U S Navy uniform waiting for an airplane to board for Hawaii when someone at the airport in San Francisco handed me a book and said read it you'll love it. He was right, it was authored by Rod McKuen and the title was *Listen to the Warm*. I fell in love with the book and read it many many times on nights when my world was caving in on me. I tried to emulate Rod McKuen and I did a fairly good job of sounding just like him. Until I realized that I needed to find my own style if I had any intention of ever becoming an author. I wrote poem after poem and journaled in between. I bought a small portable typewriter and drove everyone in my hootch nuts with its clacking at each stroke of a lettered key. I wrote a lot about the war and what my duty consisted of. Fifty years later after I retired I took up writing again. I wanted to leave a legacy so my grandkids and future great grandchildren could learn something about me and pass it on.

My 9 yr old grandson Jake has always been interested in my writing and asked a lot of questions once my books were being published. His family moved to another town, not too far from where I live and started the school year off at a new grade school. It was hard on him not knowing any of his new classmates. Eventually, he began to fit it. In his second year, the teacher offered a poetry portion of her class for the kids to try their hand at writing poetry. I attended a reading they had of their own poetry. I was amazed at how well Jake and his classmates did. As a reward, I told Jake that I would see to it that he got published.

I hope you have as much fun reading this as I did just putting the book together. I sincerely thank you from all of us. The father, the Son and the Grandson.

                    Ron Whittle

Published by Human Error Publishing
Paul Richmond
www.humanerrorpublishing.com
paul@humanerrorpublishing.com

Copyright © 2020
by
Human Error Publishing & Ron Whittle
All Rights Reserved

ISBN: 978-09991985-6-8

Front Cover: Ron Whittle
&
Human Error Publishing

Human Error Publishing asks that no part of this publication be reproduced or transmitted in any form or by any means electronic or mechanical, including photocopy, recording or information storage or retrieval system without permission in writing from Ron Whittle and Human Error Publishing . The reasons for this are to help support publisher and the artist.

The opinions in this manuscript are those of the Authors and do not reflect any of the positions of the United States Government. Any resemblance to anyone on the planet earth is a complete and utter mistake. This book is the work of nonfiction; names, characters, places, and incidents are a product of the author's imagination and it's not always coincidental that much of the book is written with others in mind. And you know who you are. All rights reserved.
To contact the Author,
Email: whittle_ron@yahoo.com

Tabel of Contents

Arthur Whittle   10

Ron Whittle   38

Jake Hansen   86

Arthur Whittle

Dapples was her last name,
given by her Pa
Roe was her first name, given by her Ma
she always felt belittled and thought it was a mistake
cuz being named after horse do do
really takes the cake

Once there was a little tadpole
His friends called him Tad
A big giant was who Tad called Dad
One day he sassed his mother
and that was really bad
Now he avoids his father,
bad Tad's Dad is mad

You'd never think it
but little Joey Crinket
Spread out his toys and trinkets
All over the front room floor
His Dad was late, stepped on a skate, and said goodbye to his mate
as he sailed thru the front door

Two little fish swimming in the lake
One had a birthday, so they made a cake
Then they lit the candles, they only had two
But when they tried to eat it
it was too soggy to chew

Two little birds up in their nest
one was chirpin', the other one took a rest
The mama was out looking for some food
Daddy bird would have helped
But wasn't in the mood

Two little pigs rolling in
the mud
One named Willie and
the other named Bud
They had a little sister named
Sweet little Rose
Not like her brothers cause
she wore clothes

The neighbors next door have a cute little child
Like a small fox terrier, but twice as wild
Caught him pulling up my flowers yesterday
So I bought him an alligator so he could play

Ten little kids marching in a row
Nine were okay, but one had to go
They passed some bushes
and that one little kid
unzipped his britches and guess what he did

Riding in the school bus waving at everyone
Just talking and bouncing is half the fun
Making faces at the kids in the car behind
Laughing with their friends, and having a great time

Peanut butter, peanut butter everywhere
I even got peanut butter in my hair
Peanut butter, peanut butter on my chair
I even got peanut butter, you know where

Our rooster will have nothing to do
with light poles by the road
Ever since he stepped on a live wire,
he crows in morse code
Whenever he goes to the henhouse,
you can hear the old hens clear
Turn off that damn rooster
so we can get some sleep in here

Olivia walks in high heels
with her pocketbook
She dances divinely and helps Mommy cook
She mixes the cookie dough,
the best no doubt
When they come out of the oven,
she gets to pass them out

Now I know where the cowboys go,
nearly every Saturday night
They'll ride along side by side
and head for the big bright light
This is the day they got their pay
and they're going to have some fun
When they party it don't take a smarty to figure it's not for everyone
By the saloon there was a full moon,
you could hear the cowboys holler
With a smiling face, they found the place
The sign that said, Bowl two strings for a dollar.

My little brother came down the sidewalk,
walking very slow
My father stood there watching him,
what he didn't know
When Dad got close to him you could barely hear him talk
My little brother had stepped in something
the dog deposited on the walk

My grandson told me as he sat upon his trike
I can go as fast as my brother on his big bike
He raced down the driveway and out in the yard
He ran into the bushes, but not very hard

I have a funny neighbor
I think he's really weird
He wears little tiny glasses and
has a big white beard
He's always hammering on things and uses lots of paint
Seems he loves to make a racket
But no one's made a complaint
Sometimes I hear him laughin'
and I start laughin' too
Even if you're a grouch at heart
His laughin' will get to you
But don't start doing any guessing or asking reasons why
He's just a crazy neighbor
just a squirley little guy

I had a friend we called Bub,
liked to dunk for apples in the tub
He had big nostrils and by gosh,
inhaled an apple a macintosh
called the Doctor by the name of Moss,
said squeeze his nose for applesauce
This should cure him and I hope
you won't let him dunk for cantaloupe

I have a grandson, cute as he can be
He's not in kindergarten, cuz he's only three
When he wears his cowboy hat, we all call him Tex
When he writes his name in the snow
He just makes an "X"

Birds chirp, boys burp
What do girls do
Horses balk, girls talk
What do Mothers do
Doves coo, Mothers too
What do Daddies do
Drink beer, hunt deer
What do Nanas do
Bunnies quake, Nanas bake
What do Grampies do
Sheep bleat, Grampies eat
Nothing else to do

Billie Bob on his birthday, got a brand new gun
Took it out and shot at a skunk just for fun
One thing he must remember if he's hunting game
Better get lots of practice, cuz a skunk has better aim

A little girl baby duck
was swimmin' in the water
Had a swimsuit on
her mother had bought her
along came a boy duck splashin' and flippin'
His mother didn't know it
but he was skinny dippin'

A whole bunch of monkeys were up in a tree
a boy monkey gave a girl monkey a little squeeze
He chased her through the jungle
and teased her some more
Then she turned around
and punched him until his snozzola got sore

A little country bumpkin, sat on a pumpkin
Playing his harmonica one day
Anyone could tell, he didn't play very well
So the old farmer chased him away

A cute little girl has a doll named "Nan-thie"
Just a plain little doll, nothing real "fan-thie"
And wherever she goes, "Nan-thie" goes too
All dressed up like big girls do

Forty seven Indians out on the plains
They'll dance around the fire unless it rains
then they will gather in a big teepee
Make some buttered popcorn and watch TV

I woke up this morning to
a little bird's song
A pretty tune but the
words were all wrong

When I buy a bag of jelly beans for my little granddaughter's sake
We set my penalties down early, three blacks for each red I take
Everyone gets a little paper cup, to put their prized selections in
The rules are,
I must spread mine out so they can snitch one now and then
You can't put anything over on Missy,
for two years old she is very bright
She can take her cup of jelly beans and explain she's a little light

1996

Arthur Whittle

Ron Whittle

We are all lost stars
trying to light up
the night sky
Some of us are just more
lost than others
and that is why
I need to hold
your hand
You seem
to know the way

The beautiful
thing is
I wasn't even
looking for you
when you found
me

I'm not sure what I'll do
if tomorrow
is the day
I've been praying for

What some people
wouldn't do
for your life
Nothing kills
faster
than a life
not lived
or a moment
not taken
A smile
not seen
and love
not given

You were art in progress
way back then
you must be a masterpiece
by now
how lucky was I
to have known you

You left
and your shadow
lingers on
in all the places
we once knew
retracing our footsteps
trying to figure out
what happened

**It's not a famous Yogi Berra quote
but rather one of my own not so famous quotes**

You don't know
What you don't know
Until you know it

Words do not always
come easily to me
most of the time they have
their way with me
and use me as a medium
to get to a piece of paper

When I thought
I finally made it home
I found out
I was only a refugee
a leftover from the war
Home had moved on
and barely remembered
my name
It's going to be
one more burial
my friends and family
will have to mourn
and one more thing I might not
be able to get over

We're just strangers now
with the same past
and I love
having you around
Even if it is only
a memory

To the dedication of windows, doors and roof shingles

The words I speak
are the foundation
to the house I
will build
with my written
words of poetry
Solid are the decks
and walls
that await the roof
that I frame
weather tight
I live within and on
the words that
are strong and
form the beams
that hold this
structure aloft
Books form the
stairways that
lead to a
loftier sense of being
and this house
becomes a
temporary home
to the wayward
and lost
that they
may someday
find their way
to lay their own
foundations and
choose to build
for the needs of the
next generation
that wishes to write
and be heard

There are only two places
where you could be
either here or there
and I haven't found you here
so you must be there
There are so many places
where there could be
Where do I start to look

There are no daffodils
or roses
not even dandelions
only jungle orchids
that few will ever see
There might have been
flowers at one time
but the war over here
pretty much ended
anything that might have
been beautiful

The stars speak to me
and sometimes I'm afraid
to listen
other times they are
shooting at me
and I don't know why

The parking meter out in the street
says we are out of time
and isn't it just my luck
to be out of quarters

The Moon
inspires most of us
and just like the moon
Sometimes I'm just so full of it

The dirt under my nails
should tell you
a lot about me
and my callous hands
could tell you
where I have been
and what I have done
should you decide
to read them
My eyes are there
for you to look into
my soul
I am an open book
to read should you
care to and
there is no need to
dogear the pages
this book is not
that long
but is worth the read

Some people have their lives
Some people have their music
I have my words to hide behind

So essential was it
that the government
needed me
to send me
to either start the
the war in earnest
or end it
one

Singing love songs in the solitude of my car

Sadness has a way
to wear my face
from time to time
and piercing the darkness
is always one point of light
It's just enough
to chase the darkness away
for a while
Fairytales do not really exist
but dreams
Well, dreams are real enough
to make you a believer
and I've had to learn
to live on less before
There always seems to be one more
illusion to preserve
in the fabric of life
And I have followed that thread
in a promise
to find an escape
that never comes
Beat up and broken
I live on to write
the next chapter in life
as most of the walking wounded do
Singing love songs in the solitude of my car
Loudly, to see if that helps
put things back into perspective

Shoulda
Coulda
Woulda

Didn't
Couldn't
Wouldn't

and regret it

Rivers of time pass
never standing still
always running like water
taking the shortest route
to the sea
Time only pauses
for that split second moment
somewhere between life and death
then resumes
as it always has
waiting for no one

Poetry is
the exchange of
black and white words
for the color images
in your mind

Once touched
I became a poet
Blessed are the touched
for they will never
be the same again
Blessed are the touched
for they will inherit the words

Once there was a world
I held it in my hands
I let go long enough
to see if it would spin
and everything
spun out of control
and I would never
hold it again

Alright so I'm not perfect
I was never perfect
and in all likelihood
will be imperfect
till the day I die
It evidently
is not one of the
better skills
I was born with

Not knowing
can be
a blessing
in disguise
and if that
is so
then I wonder
what kind
of blessing
could I be
if I knew

Not every flower that grows
is meant for someone's garden
This flower grows wild
in the midst of the city
Tough enough to grow
in the crack of an asphalt parking lot
and no one sees its beauty
for what it is
Just another weed
that grows up in the city
destined to be killed off
before it reaches maturity

Mirrors
are just
glass
with a meaningless
reflection
of someone
you might have
known at one time

Matter is matter
and that's all there
is to it
Matter happens

Like a large boulder
that is always there
It's a habit of mine
not to change too much
and not to move too far
from where I was found

It doesn't matter
which direction
you're going
as long as
you're going forward
and I would have
liked to have been
at least
leaning that way
with you

It always seems my life
is a page left unturned
or one left un-dogeared
and I'm not sure
how this story should end
I'm not sure
if I'm supposed to know
Not many will understand me
but the ones who do
will never forget me

If there was ever
a place not to look
for comfort and love
it would be in a sea
of faces that mob
the big city streets

I'd like to be able to tell you
that things will get better tomorrow
but the ugly truth is
We just get better at accepting
things the way they are

I was mistaken, I thought
there was a whole big world
out there calling my name
It was actually
a war in need of combatants

I was left to
figure it out on my own
Each man will have to
deal with it on their own terms
I am here but dream of being there
and finally got back to there
and I dream of the days I was here
and what I had to do

I was always
like the moon
Lonely
and full of self doubt
but sometimes I shone
brighter than a harvest moon
and the only one
who would believe that
is you

I think it might be
a good thing
to hold your hand
It's not for love
but for friendship
Sometimes
a friend's hand
is there to help heal
a hurting heart
especially
when it needs a hug

For my best friend
Hugs for Kathi

I have only
one goal
in my life
I just want
to be genuine

I had a flower once
it picked me
to belong to
After a couple of days
I wilted and died
and never smelled
as good as the flower

I am me
I've always been me
and no one else

I have
what I have
and I'm happy
with that

but I lost
what I lost
and I'm not all that
happy without it

it's not easy
being me

As much as I might
want to
I don't think I could
say hello
and risk having to say
another goodbye

We have to do what
we want to do now
Life like a snowflake
will refuse
to last any length of time

Jake Hansen

Yellow is happy
Yellow is bright
Yellow is the sun
Yellow is golden
Yellow tastes like a banana
Yellow smells like corn
Yellow sounds like a whistle
Yellow feels warm
Yellow looks like a leaf
Yellow makes me glad
Yellow is amazing… .

The sweet sound of the pencil screeching
Coloring cartoons with colored pencils
enormous emotions exploding through my art
taking time to do it right!
finding ways to finish my sketch...

Catastrophic Cat
Chasing a mouse
In the starry evening sky
at the home on Kelly St
because the cat wants to play...

I see leprechauns dancing.
You smell the corn beef cooking.
Listening to the parade
Tasting the cabbage at the table
Holding a four leaf clover
St Patrick's Day!

The drive there was long
It was fun at first
getting there and all
It was late in the season
and most of the rides were closed
Could not decide what to do
so we went right back home
and were waiting for next year
to try again

Screech!
The school bus just went to a halt to pick me up from school.
BANG!
Kids are slapping the seat.
Yippee!
Kids are almost home.
BEEP BEEP!
A car is slow so we can beep our horn, screech!
We are home.

Singing
Dancing
Playing
Boogieing
Feeling
Hearing
Listening

Jumping in the pool
Under the sun all day long
New summer feelings
Everyone loves June!

Hero. polite, brave, lifting, pulling
Saving people, secret, disguise, awesome
betraying, unforgiving, destroying,
mean, bad, villain...

Cuphead is my favorite game
It looks like an old 1930's cartoon!
I love to draw in that kind of style
so this is perfect for me!

Chocolate is delicious!
Delicious just for you!
You deserve a treat!
Treat yourself with...
Willy Wonka Chocolate!
Chocolate is made with care
Care with delight
Delight is another word for chocolate

Leaves fall in Autumn
Jumping in the leaves is great sport
Not too cold
not too warm
just right for Autumn fun

There was once a man from Peru
Who once dreamed about eating his shoe
Then he woke up in the middle of the night
and to his fright
He found out that his dream came true

A dog
Friendly, playful
Loving, playful, stealing
Our hearts away
Animal

Epilogue

Jake

Don't waste your youth on growing up too fast
Be the dreamer that others wish they could be
Make mistakes
Someday they will be called experience
Be the one who was told you couldn't
but you did
Refuse to be your own limitations
Remember always, you don't have to be right
but you have to be honest with yourself
and there is no comfort in being silent
when you can be the center of attention
by creating all the noise

Love you always

Gramps

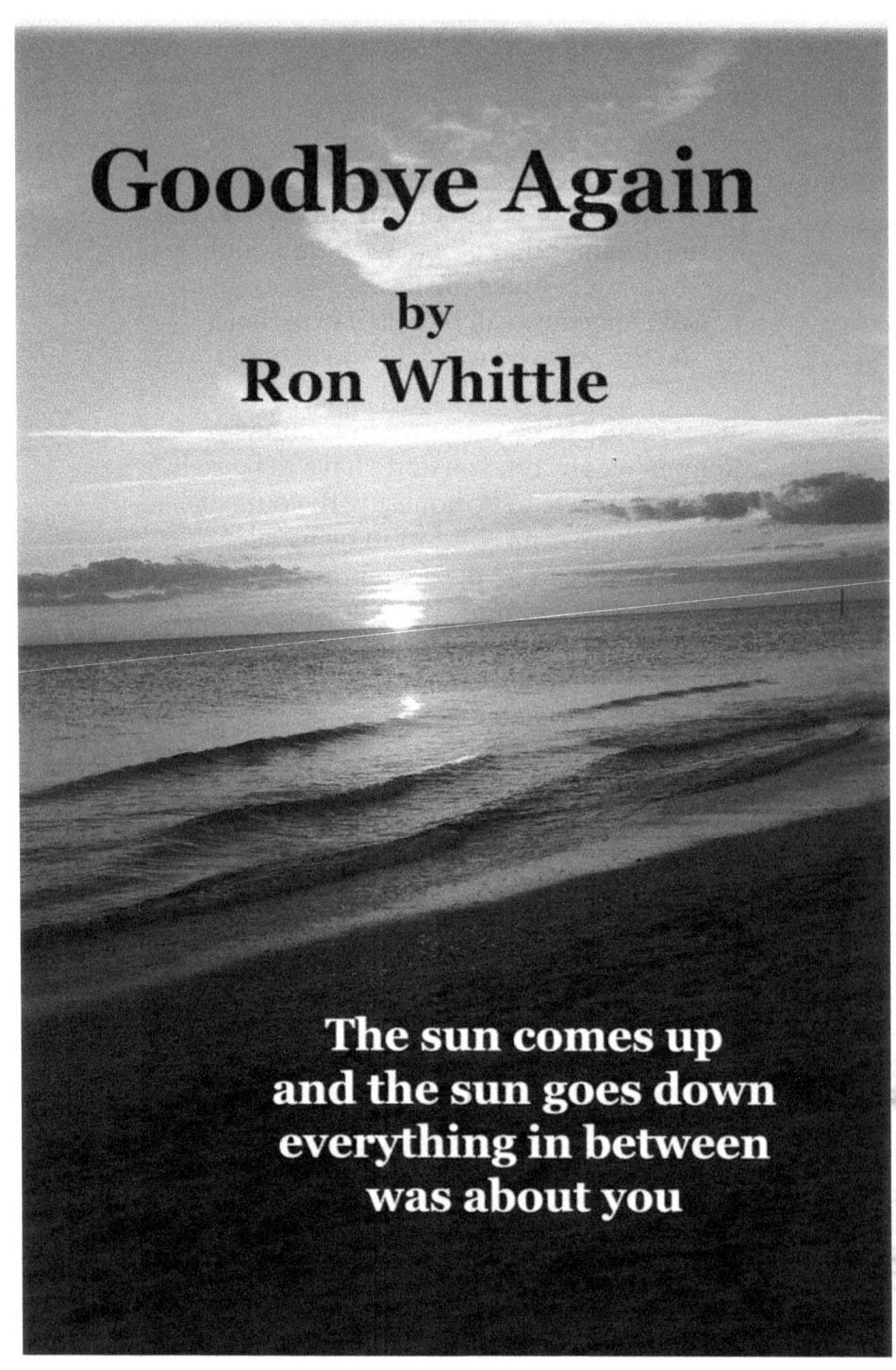

Free War Zone

Postcards from A War Zone

by
Ron Whittle

Biography for Ron Whittle

Ron Whittle born in Worcester, Ma. in 1947. Ron was educated in his home town of Shrewsbury Massachusetts Class of 1966. Further education came by way of the U.S. Navy, Veteran of the Viet Nam conflict, Apollo 13 recovery team and 45 years of family living. Ron divides his time between his home in Worcester, and the shores of Cape Cod and Rhode Island. Ron's prose is recognized as thoughtful, romantic, thought provoking, serious and funny. His wonderfully warped and quirky point of view will surely make you smile and perhaps will give you a laugh. His influences include Tom Waits, Lawrence Ferlinghetti, Edgar Allan Poe, Ogden Nash, Ezra Pound and Rod McKuen. Ron is a member in good standing in the Worcester County Poetry Association, a member of the Works in Progress/ Outlaw Stage at the Worcester Artist Group, Founding member of the Worcester Art Walk, and a member of the Warrior Writers of Boston.

Those that have enjoyed Ron's previous work, can be on the look out for future posting on face book, other E poetry sites and readings through out New England. Ron has also appeared and read on many television programs. He also appeared at the Massachusetts State Poetry Festival in Salem, Ma. Great Falls Word Festival at Turners Falls, Ma. and the Garlic Festival in Orange, Ma.. Ron's books are currently available on Amazon and at Barnes and Noble. and are internationally available.

Ron 's book "Postcards from a war zone" is a brutally honest look at the realities of love and war. Ron was a crew chief on a helicopter that serviced the Marine Corp in I Corp South Vietnam during the years 1968 to 1970. "Poems from a war zone" is a hard hitting look at war and the second book in the war zone series and the third book published by Ron. Other books in the works are multiples of chap books and more of the "again" series of books.

www.ingramcontent.com/pod-product-compliance
Lightning Source LLC
Chambersburg PA
CBHW071152090426
42736CB00012B/2304